A Mountain Lion Ate the Corn Chips

A Mountain Lion Ate the Corn Chips

Written by Leslie McGuire

Illustrated by Brian Floca

HOOKED ON
PHONICS™

Contents

Special Words

Special words help make this story fun.
Your child may need help reading them.

lion

mountain

scary

1. Let's Go Camping!

Dave and Chuck wanted to go camping.
But no one could take them.
"I have to bake," said Mom.
"I need to fix the car," said Dad.
"Now what do we do?" said Chuck.

"It's summer," said Dave. "It's hot!"

"What's the matter with Mom and Dad, anyway?" whined Chuck.

"I bet they were never bored kids like us," they grunted as they stomped back inside.

So Chuck and Dave scattered
toys all over. They made a model
airplane and got glue in their hair.
They switched channels on the TV.
They played catch with a corn muffin
for a while.

"I know what to do!" said Dave
as they brushed the muffin bits under
a chair. "Let's go camping anyway!"

"How?" asked Chuck.

"We'll put up the tent in the back
yard!" said Dave. "It will be just
as good!"

"We'll get the sleeping bags,"
said Chuck, "and maybe Dad's
camping lantern."

"We can bring snacks and drinks," said Dave.

"Let's do it!" yelled Chuck.

They got all of the stuff they needed — pillows, blankets, comics, a set of checkers, a big butterfly net (in case they got attacked by bugs), the tent, the sleeping bags, earmuffs (in case it got chilly), some rope, slippers, gumdrops, lots of soft drinks, the lantern, a bag of popcorn, a bag of corn chips, some water, a spyglass, an old trumpet (in case they would have to yell for help really loud), some sticks, as well as some plastic bags, which always come in handy. You never know.

They made a big heap and started to put up the tent.

"This is hard!" said Chuck as the rope snagged his sneaker and he tripped onto the grass.

"No, it's not," said Dave. "Just pull harder on the rope!"

But every time they pulled the rope, the tent pegs popped out.

Dad came out and said, "Let me give you a hand." He had a big hammer. He banged in the tent pegs really well.

After that, the ropes held better. Then they saw that the tent pole was lopsided.

They got up the pole — sort of — but they almost poked a hole in the top of the tent.

"Does this tent look saggy to you?" asked Dave when they were finished.

"A little, but it will be fine," said Chuck, "as long as it does not rain."

"What do you mean, rain?" asked Dave.

"Forget it," said Chuck, looking up at the sky. "It will not rain."

It was starting to get dark. They had to hurry to get all of the stuff inside the tent while they could still see.

First they put in the sleeping bags.

"Where can we put the rest of our things?" asked Chuck. "There's still a lot of stuff that needs to fit into the tent."

"We can do it," said Dave. "Just hand it all in to me. I will make it fit."

2. Bug Attack!

Mom kissed them and said, "Sleep well. Sweet dreams."

Dad hugged them and said, "Now, don't get too scared in the dark."

They were in the little tent, sitting on the sleeping bags — all alone.

"I'm not sleepy," said Chuck. "Are you?"

"No, but there's no TV out here," said Dave. "What do you want to do?"

"Let's tell a scary story," said Chuck.

"I do not think any story you make up will be very scary," said Dave.

"That's what you think," said Chuck.

He gave the lantern a push. The shadows in the tent got jagged and creepy as they flashed up and down. It looked pretty scary.

"These two boys were camping out in the forest," Chuck began, "when all of a sudden, they could hear this crackling, swishing, creepy noise! Then a yell."

"Before they could do anything, a really big mountain lion ripped into the tent, and..."

Just when Chuck was getting to the good part, the lantern went out. It was dark. It was very dark.

"Uh-oh," said Dave. "Now, just when we need to see, we cannot see a thing."

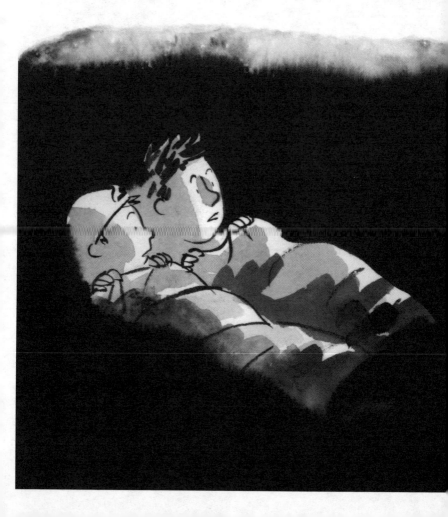

That's when there was an odd noise outside. It was a crackling, swishing, creepy noise.

"What's that?" whispered Dave.

"I do not know," said Chuck, "but it sounds big."

"Do you think maybe it's a mountain lion?" asked Dave.

Chuck wanted Dave to look. Dave said it was better if Chuck was the one to take a look.

So no one looked.

They waited. The noise stopped.

"Whatever it was," said Dave, "it's not out there anymore."

They tried to get the lantern lit again.

"What's the matter with this thing?" Chuck asked. He turned it upside down.

Dave looked at it. "I bet there's no gas left in it," he said.

"So that means we have to sit here in the dark?" asked Chuck.

"We can make a fire," said Dave. "That way, we can see. It will feel a lot more like real camping."

"How can we make a fire?" asked Chuck.

"No problem," said Dave. "Mike said you can start a fire by rubbing two sticks together."

"Let's give it a try," said Chuck, picking up the sticks.

They went out to make the fire.
But, no matter how hard they rubbed
the sticks together, they could not
make a fire.

"Oh well," said Chuck. "It's not
that dark outside the tent."

That's when there was a buzz.
Then six buzzes. Then ten!

"Ouch!" yelled Chuck.

"What?" asked Dave.

"Bug attack!" yelled Chuck. "Let's
get back in the tent!"

3. Snake Attack!

They ran inside the tent and quickly
zipped the flap shut — just in time.

"I bet there are a hundred bugs out
there," said Dave.

"Looking at all of those hungry bugs
is making me hungry," said Chuck.

"Me too," said Dave. "Let's eat the corn chips."

They got into the sleeping bags with the bag of corn chips between them.

All of a sudden, Dave jumped up.

He landed on top of Chuck.

"What are you doing?" yelled Chuck. "That hurt!"

"There's a thing in my sleeping bag!" whispered Dave.

"What kind of thing?" asked Chuck.

"A long, thin, wiggly thing," said Dave.

"How long?" asked Chuck.

"Long and wiggly, like a snake!" said Dave. His teeth were chattering so badly that he could barely say it.

"A real snake?" asked Chuck.

"Yes!" yelled Dave. "A real snake is in my sleeping bag! What do we do?"

Chuck sat thinking for a while. Then he said, "Let's throw your sleeping bag out of the tent. Then we can grab it and dump the snake on the grass."

"Good thinking," said Dave.

They unzipped the tent flap and tossed the sleeping bag out.

Then they ran back into the tent and zipped it shut.

"That way, the snake can't come back in," said Dave, panting.

"I think we should put the sleeping bag very far away from the tent," said Chuck, "just in case the snake wants to come back."

"OK," said Dave. "But let's do it fast before the snake gets out by itself!"

So they jumped out and grabbed the sleeping bag. They dragged it way over by a big tree.

"Run!" yelled Dave.

"Wait," said Chuck. "We should dump it out now!"

They held the corners of the sleeping bag and started to shake it up and down.

All of a sudden, something long and thin fell on the grass.

Dave and Chuck began to run. Then Chuck stopped.

Chuck began to snicker.

"What's so funny?" snapped Dave.

But Chuck could not say anything
yet. He had the hiccups.

"How come you are not running?"
asked Dave.

"Take a look at the—hic—scary
snake!" he said.

4. Mountain Lion Attack!

Dave went over very slowly and, bending down, he took a look.

It was a rope!

"Pretty—hic—scary rope," snickered Chuck.

Dave didn't care. He was so glad it was not a snake. He felt a lot better.

They were about to take the sleeping bag back into the tent when, all of a sudden, there was that noise.

It was the crackling, swishing, creepy noise.

"Did you hear that?" whispered Chuck.

"Yep!" hissed Dave. "It's just like the noise when the lantern went out."

"It's that big thing!" said Chuck. "It's back!"

"What happened to your hiccups?" asked Dave.

"Maybe the hiccups went away when I got scared," said Chuck.

That's when they saw a long, dark shadow crossing the yard.

It was big! It looked fuzzy! It was as big as a mountain lion, and it was right in the middle of the yard!

"Let's go back to the house!" hissed Chuck. But there was no way to get back to the house unless they went right past it!

"What is it?" whimpered Dave. "What if it's really a mountain lion?"

"I am so scared," whimpered Chuck. "Let's yell for Dad!"

"We can't!" snapped Dave. "The mountain lion will eat us before Dad gets out here!"

"We have to hide!" hissed Dave.

"Hide where?" asked Chuck.

"UP!" said Dave. He started up the tree as fast as he could go. Chuck was right in back of him.

They got up that tree faster than they had ever gotten up it before.

"What if mountain lions can get up trees?" hissed Dave.

"Do not say a word," whispered Chuck. "I bet it does not know we are here!"

"You are right!" whispered Dave. "Look! I think it's going into the tent!"

They saw the dark shape slowly stick its head into the tent. Then it went all the way in. There was thumping and bumping. There was crackling and crashing. There was snuffling and slurping.

Chuck and Dave hung onto the tree branch as hard as they could.

"I just know it's a mountain lion," sobbed Dave.

"If we were in there, we would be a mountain lion snack!" sniffled Chuck.

"Are we ever lucky," whimpered Dave. "We got up this tree just in time."

"Shhh!" hissed Dave. "It's coming back out!"

Dave and Chuck watched as the dark shape came out of the tent. It passed under the tree and crashed back into the bushes.

They sat for a while. But there were no more noises.

"Did it go away?" Chuck hissed.

"I think so," said Dave. "Did you feel a raindrop?"

5. Not Scared at All!

Quickly they dropped out of the tree and down onto the grass. Looking this way and that, they shot across the yard.

"Let's go back inside," said Dave as they ran.

Just then, there was a clap of thunder. Then rain came down in buckets.

"You said it was not going to rain!" yelled Dave. He was soaked, and so was Chuck.

"So I made a mistake!" said Chuck.

"We have to get our stuff out of the tent before we go back inside," said Dave. "I need my pillow!"

"Me, too," said Chuck. "Let's do it fast—before that mountain lion gets back!"

When they got to the tent, they saw what a mess the mountain lion had made. Things were tossed all over. The soft drinks were spilled on the blankets! The corn chip bag was empty. The popcorn bag was missing. Chuck's sleeping bag was all ripped up.

"It's lucky we were not in here!" said Chuck. "Look at what it did to my sleeping bag!"

"That mountain lion ate all of the corn chips!" moaned Dave.

"That sleeping bag could have been me!" said Chuck, looking very upset.

"Thank goodness we got up that tree in time," said Dave.

"Let's get out of here!" said Chuck.
Dave nodded.

They grabbed the pillows, but
that's when they saw something odd.

The tent was flopping in a very odd
way. Then it sagged. Then it bobbed.

"Uh-oh," said Chuck. "It's raining!"

"I know that!" snapped Dave.

Just then, a big gust of wind hit the side of the tent. The tent started to lean.

"Look out!" yelled Chuck. "The tent is getting too much water! It's going to fall down!"

Just as they jumped out, a gust of wind came. The tent fell over sideways and just missed them. Dave and Chuck made a run for the house.

They clattered up the steps and stood dripping in the hallway.

"What happened?" said Mom.

"A mountain lion came and ate the corn chips!" sobbed Dave.

"What did you say?" asked Mom.

Just then the bell rang.

Dad went to get it. It was Mr. Bender, looking very wet and upset.

"Thank you so much," he said as he came inside. "I just wanted to ask if any of you saw my dog, Puppykins?"

"I do not think so," said Mom. "What does he look like?"

"He is big and tan with long fur," said Mr. Bender. "He is just a puppy, but he is a very big puppy."

"Does he look sort of like a mountain lion?" asked Chuck.

"That's him!" said Mr. Bender.

"He was in the yard just when it started to rain," said Dave.

"He ran off," said Chuck.

"Good," said Mr. Bender. "I will go see if he is back home by now."

"Now what were you saying?" asked Mom after Mr. Bender left. "Something about a mountain lion eating corn chips?"

"We did not say anything like that," said Dave after giving Chuck a sharp poke with his elbow. "There are no mountain lions here."

"So did you get scared out there?" asked Dad, with a little smile.

"Nope," said Chuck. "We just had to come in because it was raining."

"Besides," said Dave, "there is nothing to be scared of in the yard!"

"I see," said Dad.

"You are very brave," said Mom. "But it's late, so go on up to bed."

"Sleep well," said Dad.

"Sweet dreams," said Mom.

"You bet," said Chuck and Dave. "We'll clean up when the rain stops!"

There's something hidden under the sand of the Rub' al-Khali desert on the Arabian Peninsula. Nicholas Clapp is determined to find it. But the desert is the size of Texas. That's a whole lot of sand for one man to dig through.

1

The Lost City

What's Clapp looking for? A legendary city called Ubar. It was said to be paradise on earth. But almost 2,000 years ago it vanished without a trace.

The Search

Since 1932, explorers have crisscrossed
the desert looking for the lost city.
All they found was a wide path in the
sand that seemed to lead nowhere.

Mission: Ubar

Then, in the 1980s, Clapp came up with an unusual plan to find the lost city. And he knew just where to turn for help: rocket science!

The Question

How would modern technology help
Clapp locate the ancient city beneath
the desert? Why are some people so
obsessed with uncovering the past?

PREVIEW PHOTOS

PAGES 1, 2–3: The Rub' al-Khali desert stretches across four nations—Saudi Arabia, Oman, Yemen, and the United Arab Emirates.

PAGES 4–5: Illustration of a NASA satellite photographing Earth from space in 1999

Book Design: Red Herring Design/NYC **Photo Credits:** Photographs © 2012: age fotostock: 45 bottom (Guylain Doyle), 42 top center (Value Stock Images); Alamy Images: 10 (Carolyn Clarke), 42 top right (Gaba/G&B Images), 42 bottom (ImageDJ), 38 top (Jeff Morgan), 43 top left (James Quine), 43 bottom right (Peter Widmann); American Museum of Natural History: 40; AP Images/Pat Sullivan: 27; Bridgeman Art Library International Ltd., London/New York/Albert Bierstadt/Butler Institute of American Art, Youngstown, OH/Gift of Joseph C. Butler III 1946: 19 bottom; Corbis Images: 38 bottom (James L. Amos), 19 top (Dave G. Houser), 23 (Ali Jarekji/Reuters), 34 (George Steinmetz), 26, 37 (Kurt-Michael Westermann); David Lindroth, Inc.: 12 foreground; Dreamstime.com/Frenta: back cover foreground; George Ollen: 14; Getty Images: back cover background, cover (Thomas Northcut), 2, 3 (Slow Images), 17 (World Perspectives); iStockphoto/DHuss: 45 center; Kay Chernush Photography: 20; © Kristen Mellon: 36; Media Bakery: 32; NASA: 4, 5 (Goddard Space Flight Center and U.S. Geological Survey), 24 (JPL), 12 background (SeaWiFS Project/Goddard Space Flight Center/ORBIMAGE); National Geographic Stock/James L. Stanfield: 30; NEWSCOM: 18 background, 19 background (Agencia el Universal/El Universal de Mexico), 45 top (Cindy Miller Hopkins/DanitaDelimont.com); Royal Geographical Society/B. Thomas: 13; ShutterStock, Inc.: 8 (Marilyn Barbone), 42 top left (BW Folsom), 43 bottom left (Andreas Gradin), 43 top right (R. Mackay), 1 (David Steele), 39 (stocksnapp); Sipa Press/Clapp/Hedges/Ollen: 33; Superstock, Inc.: 43 bottom center (F1 ONLINE), 18 top (Robert Harding Picture Library); The Granger Collection, New York: 18 bottom; Yale University/John Darnell/The Theban Desert Road Survey: 28, 29 foreground, 29 background.

Library of Congress Cataloging-in-Publication Data
Rinaldo, Denise.
Lost city spotted from space! : is an ancient land under the sand?
/ Denise Rinaldo.
p. cm.
Includes bibliographical references and index.
ISBN-13: 978-0-545-32929-3
ISBN-10: 0-545-32929-9
1. Ubar (Extinct city)—Juvenile literature. 2. Excavations (Archaeology)—Oman—Ubar (Extinct city)—Juvenile literature. I. Title.
DS247.O63R56 2012
939'.49—dc22
2011009891

Lost City Spotted From Space!

Is an Ancient Land Under the Sand?

DENISE RINALDO

THE LEGENDARY ancient city of Ubar was said to be the world's largest supplier of frankincense (above), a type of incense.

1

Paradise Lost?

Did a legendary city disappear?
Or did it never exist?

The year is 1932. Bertram Thomas, a British explorer, has been trekking for days through the Rub' al-Khali. That's a vast desert on the Arabian Peninsula. "Look!" says Thomas's guide. The guide is pointing to a wide path in the sand. "There's the road to Ubar!"

Thomas knew the story well. Ubar was once a rich, beautiful trading city. A powerful king had built it. He wanted it to be a paradise on Earth. It became the world's

The Rub' al-Khali

The Rub' al-Khali desert is one of the largest sand deserts in the world. It covers about 230,000 square miles and has sand dunes high enough to be called mountains.

SYRIA

IRAQ

IRAN

KUWAIT

Persian Gulf

Gulf of Oma

SAUDI ARABIA

QATAR

UNITED ARAB EMIRATES

OMAN

Red Sea

Rub' al-Khali Desert

Shisur (Ubar)

Arab Sea

SUDAN

ERITREA

YEMEN

Gulf of Aden

12

largest supplier of frankincense. That's a kind of incense made from the sap of a local tree. It was used in perfume, medicine, and embalming (preserving dead bodies). In the ancient world, it was as valuable as gold.

Buried Treasure

According to legend, the people of Ubar became wealthy from their trade in frankincense. They also became greedy and prideful. It was said that God was so angry with them that he made the city vanish beneath the sands.

Thomas didn't turn down the path that day. The goal of his journey was to become the first European to cross the Rub' al-Khali desert. He was afraid he wouldn't make it if he went chasing after a legend.

Still, he took careful notes about the location of the road his guide had shown him.

BERTRAM THOMAS (center) with a group of Arabian warriors

NICHOLAS CLAPP set out to prove that the legendary city of Ubar really did exist.

2

One Man's Obsession

Nicholas Clapp finds a surprising partner for his search for Ubar.

Flash forward to California in the 1980s. A man named Nicholas Clapp had become obsessed with Ubar. Clapp is a filmmaker. He's also an amateur archeologist. Archeology is the scientific study of ancient peoples and the objects they left behind.

Clapp had read everything he could about the legendary city. He'd learned about it in an old book of stories called *The Book of the One Thousand and One*

Nights. He read about the city in writings from ancient Rome. He also discovered that Ubar is mentioned in the Koran, the Muslim holy book. And he carefully read Bertram Thomas's story about the road to Ubar. He pored over ancient maps. And he became convinced that Ubar was real.

Clapp decided to plan an expedition to find the lost city. But the Rub' al-Khali desert is huge—the size of Texas. How could he narrow his search?

Search Party in Space

As he planned his expedition, Clapp had an unlikely partner in mind: NASA, the U.S. space agency.

Clapp called NASA. "I'd like to talk to someone about using the space shuttle to find a lost city," Clapp said.

What was he thinking?

NASA's mission is to explore space. But it also studies Earth from space. Scientists use spacecraft equipped with high-tech cameras to take photos of the planet. And some of NASA's imaging technology

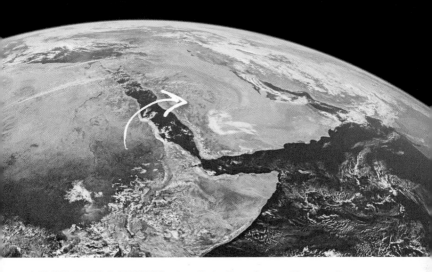

TAKEN FROM A SATELLITE, this digitally enhanced image shows a view of the Arabian Peninsula from space.

can actually see through sand.

When Clapp told NASA scientists about Ubar, they were fascinated—and they wanted to help. As one researcher said to Clapp, "What's science for, if not to find out what exists or doesn't?" So NASA researchers took photos of the Rub' al-Khali desert from outer space. Then they searched the images for evidence of Ubar.

The images didn't show signs of a lost city. But they did show a long, wide road under the desert. Maybe it was the road to Ubar, covered by drifting sands!

Hit the Road

Through the ages, these famous roads have connected people and places.

The Appian Way

This was the earliest and the best known of the great military roads of ancient Rome. The first portion of the road was built in 312 BCE. It stretched 130 miles, from Rome to Capua, in present-day Italy. The original road base was made of heavy stone blocks and may have been covered with gravel.

The Silk Road

This ancient trade route was actually a system of interlinked roads that connected China with traders throughout the Middle East.

Camel caravans traveled these routes to exchange Chinese silk, jade, and gold in return for goods such as wool and silver. The Silk Road opened up in the second century BCE and was used for more than 1,700 years.

El Camino Real
Spanish for "the Royal Road." This series of footpaths was built between 1769 and 1823 in California. The roads linked Spanish villages and outposts from San Diego to Sonoma. Along the route, the Spanish built 21 missions where they tried to convert Native Americans to Christianity.

The Oregon Trail
Difficult and dangerous, this route stretched for 2,000 miles across North America. From 1843 to 1869, more than half a million pioneers walked or rode along the trail to reach a new life in Washington, Oregon, and California. One in ten of the pioneers died along the way, mostly from disease.

PROFESSOR JURIS ZARINS (standing) was one of the experts who joined Clapp on his expedition to find Ubar.

3

Dream Team

Explorers on the ground get help from outer space.

Nicholas Clapp now had enough evidence to convince experts to join an expedition to the Rub' al-Khali. His team included Juris Zarins, an archeology professor with years of experience in the Arabian desert. Clapp also recruited Ranulph Fiennes, a man described by the *Guinness Book of World Records* as the world's greatest living explorer.

Using ancient documents, plus the NASA

information, the team chose five places to search. All were in Oman—a desert nation on the Arabian Peninsula. In the summer of 1990, the team traveled to the Rub' al-Khali. The search had begun.

Where's Ubar?

Clapp's team spent two weeks in the scorching desert. They decided to skip one of the five spots they had originally chosen to search. It was near a tiny town called Shisur. They thought it was an unlikely spot for a major trading center.

So where was Ubar? The team left Oman without an answer. But they planned to return in a few months to resume the search.

A short time later, however, war came to the Middle East. The nation of Iraq invaded its neighbor Kuwait. The explorers had to postpone their return to Oman.

As the war in the Middle East raged, Clapp's team received new images from NASA. Those images totally changed their strategy.

IN 1990, CLAPP'S TEAM **left the Rub' al-Khali
desert without finding Ubar**

THIS IMAGE of the Rub' al-Khali desert was taken by NASA astronauts. The thin pink streaks show ancient roads leading to an area that Clapp thought might be the site of Ubar.

4

Desert Hub

All roads lead to Ubar.

The NASA images were amazing. They showed ancient roads buried beneath the Rub' al-Khali desert. The roads came from different directions and met at one center point, like spokes on a wheel meeting at the hub.

Clapp imagined long camel trains of traders traveling along the spokes and meeting up at a great trading center—Ubar!

In 1991, the United States invaded Iraq and the war in Kuwait came to an end. Clapp's team headed for the spot where the roads in the NASA images came together. It was Shisur—the tiny desert village that the team had decided not to visit during their first trip.

Asking for Directions

When Clapp arrived in Shisur, he asked a man whether he knew where Ubar was. The man said he didn't. But he added, "Maybe not far away." Then he pointed to a spot in the distance. There are some ruins there, he told Clapp. But they were not Ubar. They were the remains of a 500-year-old fort.

Ubar, if it ever existed, had disappeared around 300 CE. It would be thousands of years old—not hundreds.

Still, the team decided to investigate the ruins. They had brought along an incredible tool. They called it the red sled. It's a radar device that can detect objects underground. (Radar is a technology used to locate things by bouncing radio waves off them.) By dragging the red sled across the ground, team members could get a rough picture of what lay beneath.

THE RED SLED, a radar device like this one, was used to detect what might be under the ruins near Shisur.

Wandering the Desert

In Egypt, two explorers discover another lost city.

Egypt's Western Desert is blistering hot. Fierce sandstorms batter the area every spring. Years can pass without any rain.

It seemed like an odd place to go looking for an ancient city.

John and Deborah Darnell are specialists in a field they call desert-road archeology. In 1992, they started exploring ancient caravan roads that once led through the Western Desert. They spent years picking through artifacts. The archeologists studied bits of broken pottery along the roads. They hoped to learn about the cultures of the people who had traveled there.

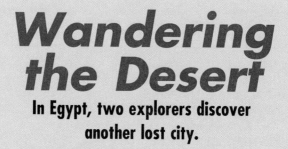

AN EXPLORING TEAM digs at the site of the ancient city in Egypt's Western Desert. John Darnell (inset) and his wife, Deborah Darnell, led the expedition.

In 2005, the Darnells discovered something huge—the ruins of a city that was more than 3,500 years old! They found a bakery that could produce "enough bread to feed an army," according to John Darnell. And they found evidence of desert soldiers who used to fight for the Egyptian pharaohs.

The Darnells believe the city was built to control the trade routes that led to an Egyptian kingdom in the Nile Valley. "We were really shocked," says John Darnell. Building a city in the middle of the desert is another example of "the incredible organizational abilities of the Egyptians."

THE RUINS OF AN ANCIENT CITY were revealed as Clapp's team excavated the site.

5

Big Dig!

Have the explorers found the hidden city at last?

The red sled detected something 30 feet below the surface. It looked like a stone well. That was interesting, but what did it mean?

There was only one way to find out. Dig!

Some of Juris Zarins's students arrived to help. Within days, they found important artifacts—objects created by humans, often long ago. There were broken pots thousands of years old. Some had been

ARCHEOLOGISTS USE SIFTER SCREENS like this to separate dirt from bits of artifacts.

made far away, in Syria and Greece. The team knew they had found the home of an ancient people who had traded with foreigners. *Like the people of Ubar.*

Staying Calm

Next the diggers uncovered a wall, then a tower. Soon the outline of an eight-sided fortress was revealed. A 30-foot tower had stood at each corner. The fortress had enclosed a small city. Inside the walls, team members found unusual artifacts. They discovered tools that had been used to turn tree sap into frankincense. *And Ubar was famous for its frankincense.*

"The pieces were fitting," Clapp later told *People* magazine. "But we didn't want to jump up and down and shout, 'Ubar! Ubar!' We were afraid we might break the spell."

THE TEAM uncovered the walls of an eight-sided fortress.

THE LAYOUT OF THE RUINS at Shisur matched the descriptions of Ubar in ancient texts.

6

Paradise Found!

Modern technology uncovers ancient history.

Had the team found Ubar? Almost certainly. The layout of the walled city matched the legends. And the site dated from when Ubar would have existed.

The archeologists also found evidence of the trade caravans that had traveled to and from Ubar. They found buried remains of campfires at hundreds of sites around the city. The campfires marked the places where traders had spent the night before

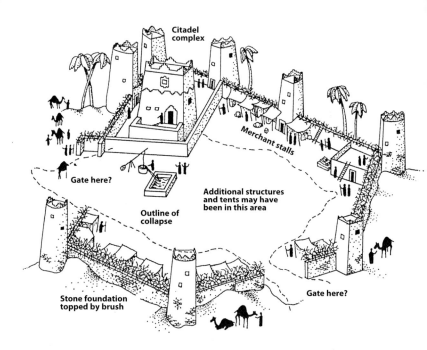

THIS ILLUSTRATION SHOWS what Ubar might have looked like. It included a fortress surrounded by a wall connecting eight or more towers.

heading back out across the desert.

Even the way the city had disappeared echoed the ancient legends. Ubar really had sunk into the earth. The dig revealed a huge limestone cavern under the walled city. Scientists think the city was destroyed when it collapsed into the cavern, which had probably once been filled with water.

Brain Power

After thousands of years, the legendary city had finally been found. NASA's technology had helped solve the ancient mystery. But according to Professor Zarins, the success of the mission was the result of something much more basic, "Brains!" By putting their heads together to make sense of evidence from a huge variety of sources, the team members had made a historic discovery. ✖

THE RUINS OF UBAR

Gridding the Site

During a dig, archeologists keep track of where every artifact is found. Here's how they do it.

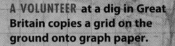

A VOLUNTEER at a dig in Great Britain copies a grid on the ground onto graph paper.

1. Create a grid of equal-sized squares on the ground. It should look like a giant piece of graph paper. Give each square its own number.

2. Now copy this grid onto a piece of graph paper. Each square on the paper represents a square on the dig site.

3. When an artifact is found, label it with the number of the square in which it was found. On the graph paper, note where the artifact was found.

4. Later, you can consult the graph paper to see where each artifact was found. And archeologists in the future can consult these grids to review the history of the dig.

AN ARCHEOLOGIST grids a site on Easter Island in the southeastern Pacific Ocean. She measures each square carefully and uses string and wooden stakes to create a grid.

FILES

Lost Civilizations

Archeologist Luca Casparis digs up the past—literally.

How did you decide to become an archeologist?

LUCA CASPARIS: Between the ages of five and ten, I was really into dinosaurs. When I was 11 or 12, I realized people were a lot more interesting.

On family trips, I'd drag my parents to archeological sites. I read all the time. *National Geographic* was a big influence on me, especially pictures of Mayan temples in the jungles of Mexico. By the time I was 12, I knew I wanted to be an archeologist. And I knew I wanted to work in Mexico.

LUCA CASPARIS is a researcher at the American Museum of Natural History. He helped dig up Monte Alban, an ancient city in Mexico that was part of the Zapotec culture.

What's the best part of your job?
CASPARIS: The fieldwork. You try to come up with a good picture of what life was like and what people did. It's very slow and very detailed, and it's also very exciting.

What is the most amazing thing you've found?
CASPARIS: We were excavating a temple that was built of adobe [clay] bricks. In one area we found a whole set of human footprints—from people who'd built the temple 1,500 years ago! It must have rained one day while they were working and the clay got wet. It was such a direct connection to people back then.

Did you put your feet in the footprints?
CASPARIS: Of course! I'm a size 12 shoe, and they were about a size eight. People were shorter back then.

Is your work ever dangerous?
CASPARIS: No, Oaxaca [a state in Mexico] is fairly safe. The only major danger in the area is killer bees. There are snakes, and there are tarantulas, but other than that, we've never had any problems.

Do local people work on the dig with you?
CASPARIS: Yes, and it's great because they're the descendants of the people who built the city. They have a direct connection and direct knowledge. Sometimes we'll find an artifact and be puzzled by it. They'll say, "Oh, yeah. You use it for water. My grandfather had one."

What's your advice for people who are thinking about a career in archeology?
CASPARIS: Read a lot and learn a foreign language. Visit archeological sites and museums. When you get to high school, volunteer on a dig. There is archeology going on in every state. Half of what I know I learned in the field. It's not just the books.

Digging in the Dirt

Here's a look at some of an archeologist's tools of the trade.

1 Flat trowel The most important tool on many digs. Use it to carefully scrape away layer after layer of earth.

2 Large pick Use this to loosen soil at the beginning of a dig. But don't just swing away. Work carefully so you don't destroy important artifacts.

3 Hand pick This small tool is good for delicate jobs.

4 Household tools You'll need everyday objects like toothpicks, toothbrushes, and spoons to uncover artifacts.

5 Sifter screen This tool separates dirt from tiny bits of broken artifacts.

6 Tape measure
Want to know how
tall that ancient wall
is? You'll need a good
tape measure.

7 Sledgehammer
Use this to break up
large rocks at the
beginning of a dig.

8 First aid kit
You'll need sun-
screen, bandages,
antiseptic for cuts,
and medicine in
case you're bitten
by a poisonous
spider or snake.

**9 Whisk broom
and dust pan**
The whisk broom is
for brushing away
dirt from your finds.
The dust pan collects
the dirt so you can
sift it for small
artifacts.

43

Hidden Cities

>> Lost: Troy

According to mythology, the ancient Greeks destroyed Troy at the end of the Trojan War.

The war started when Paris, a Trojan prince, fell in love with Helen, the wife of a Greek king. The couple fled to Troy, followed by Helen's furious husband, along with 100,000 soldiers and 1,000 ships. The Greeks destroyed Troy by sneaking through the city gates inside a giant, hollow wooden horse. The Greek writer Homer told this story in a long poem called *The Iliad*. But did the city ever really exist?

>> Lost: Pompeii

Pompeii was a busy seaside city in the Roman Empire. Wealthy people from Rome spent their summers there. But in 79 CE, a volcano called Mount Vesuvius erupted. It buried Pompeii under a thick blanket of ash. Centuries passed, and most people forgot about the city.

>> Lost: Vilcabamba

From about 1200 to 1572, the Inca Empire controlled most of western South America. They had an advanced culture, rich agriculture, and a strong government. They built an elaborate system of roads and created beautiful art and architecture.

Starting in 1532, Spanish conquistador Francisco Pizarro conquered much of the empire. A leader named Manco Inca and thousands of his followers fled to the mountain city of Vilcabamba. From there, they fought the Spanish for about 30 years.

No one knew whether these ancient cities actually existed—until archeologists uncovered them.

>> Found: In modern-day Turkey

In 1871, Heinrich Schliemann found the ruins of a city in present-day Turkey. Archeologists later discovered that nine cities had been built on the same site over 2,500 years. The seventh one dates from around 1200 BCE. That's when the Trojan War would have taken place. And the ruins show that the city really *was* destroyed in a war.

>> Found: In modern-day Italy

Throughout history, farmers living near Mount Vesuvius have found artifacts that appear to have come from Pompeii. In 1748, archeologists began to dig up the city. Volcanic ash had preserved many buildings and artifacts. Today, visitors can walk on the ancient streets of Pompeii and see what life was like in the Roman Empire.

>> Found: Machu Picchu, in modern-day Peru

In 1911, American explorer Hiram Bingham set out to find Vilcabamba. Instead, he stumbled upon Machu Picchu, the ruins of a mountaintop city of temples and palaces. Bingham later discovered the ruins of Vilcabamba, but that city was not as spectacular as Machu Picchu.

Here's a selection of books and websites for more information about archeology and lost cities.

What to Read Next

NONFICTION

Allison, Amy. *Machu Picchu*. San Diego: Lucent Books, 2003.

Caselli, Giovanni. *In Search of Troy: One Man's Quest for Homer's Fabled City*. New York: Peter Bedrick, 2001.

Clapp, Nicholas. *The Road to Ubar: Finding the Atlantis of the Sands*. Boston: Houghton Mifflin, 1998.

Deem, James M. *Bodies From the Ash: Life and Death in Ancient Pompeii*. Boston: Houghton Mifflin, 2005.

McIntosh, Jane. *Archeology* (Eyewitness Books). New York: DK Publishing, 2000.

Rinaldo, Daniel. *Cities of the Dead: Finding Lost Civilizations*. New York: Franklin Watts, 2008.

Stefoff, Rebecca. *Finding the Lost Cities*. New York: Oxford University Press, 1997.

Weil, Ann. *The World's Most Amazing Lost Cities*. Chicago: Raintree, 2012.

FICTION

Dahl, Michael. *The Worm Tunnel: A Finnegan Zwake Mystery*. New York: Pocket Books, 1999.

Erickson, John R. *Discovery at Flint Springs*. New York: Viking, 2004.

McCaughrean, Geraldine. *One Thousand and One Arabian Nights*. New York: Oxford University Press, 2000.

Websites

Archeology for Kids
www.nps.gov/archeology/ public/kids

This site explains all you need to know about the field of archeology, and it has tons of tips on how to experiment with it yourself.

Discovery Channel: Pompeii, the Last Day
http://dsc.discovery.com/ convergence/pompeii/ pompeii.html

Read about the last day of Pompeii and learn about ongoing excavations at the ancient site.

NOVA Online: Lost City of Arabia
www.pbs.org/wgbh/nova/ubar

This site details the search for Ubar and includes an interview with Professor Juris Zarins.

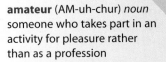

amateur (AM-uh-chur) *noun* someone who takes part in an activity for pleasure rather than as a profession

ancient (AYN-shunt) *adjective* very old

archeology (ar-kee-OL-uh-jee) *noun* the study of past cultures by looking at ancient buildings, artifacts, and human remains

artifact (ART-uh-fakt) *noun* an object made or changed by humans

caravans (KA-ruh-vanz) *noun* groups of people or vehicles that are traveling together

civilization (siv-ih-luh-ZAY-shuhn) *noun* a highly developed and organized society

descendant (di-SEND-uhnt) *noun* the child, grandchild, etc. of an ancestor

excavation (ek-skuh-VAY-shun) *noun* the process of digging up and recovering artifacts and other clues about people of the past

expedition (ek-spuh-DISH-uhn) *noun* a long journey for a special purpose, such as exploring

hub (HUHB) *noun* the center of a place or activity

incense (IN-senss) *noun* a substance that is burned to give off a pleasant smell

legendary (LEJ-uhnd-dar-ee) *adjective* describing a story that has been passed down from earlier times and that has not been proven to be true

obsessed (uhb-SESST) *adjective* fixated on one thing

peninsula (puh-NIN-suh-luh) *noun* a piece of land that sticks out from a larger landmass and is almost completely surrounded by water

sap (SAP) *noun* the liquid that flows through a plant, carrying water and food from one part of the plant to another

scorching (SKORCH-ing) *adjective* extremely hot

strategy (STRAT-uh-jee) *noun* a plan for achieving a goal

trek (TREK) *verb* to make a slow, difficult journey

INDEX

METRIC CONVERSIONS

Feet to meters: 1 ft is about 0.3 m
Miles to kilometers: 1 mi is about 1.6 km
Pounds to kilograms: 1 lb is about 0.45 kg
Acres to Hectares: 1 acre is about 0.405 ha